The Tail of Ben, the Laughtersaurus

The Brothers Grin

Indy Rishi Singh
Oshri Liron Hakak

BUTTERFLYON BOOKS

The Tail of Ben, the Laughtersaurus
Created by Oshri Liron Hakak and Indy Rishi Singh

Published by Butterflyon Books
Los Angeles
ISBN 978-1-964420-03-5

For Sofia...
Ben was born in your heart and mind,
we appreciate you and know
that he'll help many unwind.
(What a way to be kind!)

Different Kinds of Laughs

Bray - a loud, harsh laugh

Cachinnation - a loud and convulsive laugh

Cackle - a loud laugh that sounds like a chicken

Chuckle - a gentle laugh

Chortle - a gentle laugh

Giggle - a silly laugh

Guffaw - a full and hearty laugh

Snicker - a disrespectful laugh

Titter - a nervous laugh

Laughter in Different Languages

Amharic - sak'i

Arabic - dahik

Armenian - tsitsagh

Cherokee - uyetsasgv

Chinese - xiào shēng

Filipino - tawa

French - rire

Hawaiian - ʻakaʻaka

Hebrew - tschok

Hindi - hansee

Hmong- luag

Lakota - ehate

Navajo - dloh

Punjabi - hāsā

Russian - smekh

Spanish - risa

Tamil - sirippu

Thai - Ŝeīyng ḫawreāa

Turkish - kahkaha

Vietnamese - Tiếng cười

Welsh - chwerthin

Zulu - ukuhleka

Ben's Ancient Agreements of Laughter

***

Laughter is so powerful and real,
we have to treat it like a big deal.
Always laugh WITH others,
never AT sisters and brothers.
If you're sitting on the fence,
avoid laughing if it's at someone's expense.
We use laughter to help not hurt,
using it as a healing art
that helps to sooth and tend our hearts.

***

We all want to be aware
of time and place to laughter air.
Some situations need our quiet and solemnity,
in which we can breathe slowly, deeply.
Doing that can add some gentle lightness,
and helps us and others to release our tightness.
(And if we really need to laugh,
we can learn to giggle inside to avoid a gaffe.)

***

If you're eating something yummy,
remember to chew it before it gets to your tummy.
No laughing out loud
when there is food in our mouth!

The Tail of Ben,
the Laughtersaurus

The first time Ben laughed
was with his friend the tree.
He he he he he!
What a pleasant way to be!
The tree gifted Ben a leaf for his tail
to carry the memory,
of the laughter they shared together
that filled them both with glee.
And that's how Ben
became a Laughtersaurus.
Here's his tale…
I promise it won't bore us…

A big giant rock was headed for earth,
but Ben the Laughtersaurus
was ready with mirth.

My laughter will protect us!
My laughter is infectious!
My laughter will make a healing sphere,
softening all that might affect us!

The creatures crowded around Ben,
and when the big rock bumped
and shook a seismic ten,
all were safe who had taken shelter
in Ben's roomy laughter den.

"The life recovering from this comet…
now we will go forth and calm it.
Together we'll roam!
The Earth we'll comb!
Sail across the ocean's foam!
Laughter guides us to our inner home,
and we'll teach all sorts of creatures to laugh.
Yes! Laughter guides us on our homeward path!
With our laughter we make a safe and cozy dome…
and we will share our lovely laughter poem…"

"With a *ho ho ho*! And a *ha ha ha*!
I relax my totally wound up jaw!
A *he he he* and a *hoo hoo hoo*!
You can be a laughtersaurus too!
Join our crew
or do something new…
It'll be the most fun you ever knew!

And when it feels we're down to the very last straw,
we say *he he he hoo hoo ha ha*!

When harm comes near,
we all get clear.
We channel our fear
and call out with cheer like a seer:

He he ho ho
Danger? Oh, no!
Come here, get low
He he ho ho!
Laugh with me my sisters and my bros!
He he he ho ho ho ho!"

Over time laughter transformed
the laughing laughtersauri—
and my, O my, O my, O my—
they got so big and clear, heads held so high,
they started to blend in with the very big whole sky!

The thing with laughter
(when we keep our mind on now
and not before or after)
is it makes time go faster, faster and faster…

Time flies by, and we hold still.
Our laughter holds us in a way
that time can feel unreal!
It's good for our health,
though it's not very stealth…
(Unless we're laughing so hard,
we pull the silent laughter card.)

So what happened to Ben
and the ancient laughtersaurus crew?
Here's a thing I think
might just surprise you!

Ever listen to the laughter
of the breeze through the trees?

Or the giggles in the trickles
of the water in the streams?

Take a listen,
if you feel you're missin'
Ben and all his friends!

Hear them laughing (and girraffing)
across the Earth's ends!

"With a *ho ho ho*! And a *ha ha ha*!
I relax my totally wound up jaw!
A *he he he* and a *hoo hoo hoo*!
You can be a laughtersaurus too!
Join our crew
or do something new…
It'll be the most fun you ever knew!

And when it feels we're down to the very last straw,
we say *he he he hoo hoo ha ha*!

When harm comes near,
we all get clear.
We channel our fear
and call out with cheer like a seer:

He he ho ho
Danger? Oh, no!
Come here, get low
He he ho ho!
Laugh with me my sisters and my bros!
He he he ho ho ho ho!"

The Mend

Questions for Conversation

- Who do I laugh with the most?

- Who do I normally not laugh with, but I would like to?

- When was the most I have ever laughed?

- What's a situation where laughter or playfulness improved my mood or mindset?

Practice Being a Laughtersaurus

Power Laughter...

When we are feeling scared and sour,
here is a way to feel our power:
Stand with your feet wide apart,
arms high in the air, up with your heart.
Let the laughs burst out into the world
and feel the power from the swirl!

Quiet Laughter...

There are times where we must be silent,
maybe in a library or someplace not very vibrant.
That's when we can giggle quietly.
Without noise, we can laugh silently.
Along with your smile, some silent haa's and hee's...
or some hoohoo's if you please,
for your heart's joy and ease.

Have a Sigh, Have a Laugh, Have a Walk

Here are some simple laughter tools, backed by science.
Try them with friends, family, teachers, students, and clients…

What if we are feeling down and needing to cry?
Sometimes it helps to breathe deeply and to sigh.

"A forced sigh can regulate the nervous and respiratory systems."

"The Integrative Role of the Sigh in Psychology, Physiology, Pathology, and Neurobiology"
by Jan-Marino Ramirez
Progress in Brain Research, 2014

Remember too, if you get low,
the best medicine can be a big jolly belly HOHO!

"Laughing with the belly increases production of immune cells and thus improves immune
system functioning."

"The Effect of Mirthful Laughter on Stress and Natural Killer Cell Activity"
by Mary P Bennett, Janice M Zeller, Lisa Rosenberg, Judith McCann
Alternative Therapies in Health and Medicine, 2003

Find a loved one to hug…
and give them a giant laughter hug.

"Hugging reduces Cortisol (the "stress" hormone) levels supports healthier aging."

"4 Important New Discoveries About Hugging"
by Sebastian Ocklenburg
Psychology Today, 2022

If we are feeling frustrated and stuck,
we can start walking (and quack like a duck?)

"Walking activates the cardiovascular system and moves nutrients throughout the body and
rain, improving metabolism and coordination between the brain's hemispheres."

"Further Evidence for the Benefits of Walking"
by Miriam E Nelson, Sara C Folta
The American Journal of Clinical Nutrition, 2009

The Original Drawing of Ben, the Laughtersaurus,
by Diana Cantú-Reyna

About Cosmic Labyrinth

Indy Rishi Singh is a Founder of Cosmic Labyrinth, and we wanted to tell you about it.

Cosmic Labyrinth is a collective of educators reimagining education for the inner children in everyone. Join Cosmic Labyrinth in healing the 4 elements within our bodies and in the world.

Fire: Cosmic Labyrinth produces gatherings that bring people, animals, plants, and fungus together to regenerate our ecosystems and our people systems

Water: Join a coalition of healers, builders, artists, engineers, and doers solving problems around healthcare, agriculture, and local economics

Earth: The Cosmic Labyrinth metasystem networks and incubates small businesses, edutainment products and toys, nonprofit enterprises and more

Air: We are building a collective mythology that honors the spiritualities, mythologies, and sacred traditions of the past and present while cocreating a narrative story of resilience, abundance, and possibility for the future

Enter the Labyrinth at

www.CosmicLabyrinth.world

Children's Mental Health Toolbox

Oshri has been developing a Children's Mental Health Toolbox with NAMI Westside LA. This resource contains various materials to help children navigate their social-emotional landscapes, develop thriving mental health, and cultivate resilience, compassion and joy. The toolbox includes affirmation coloring sheets, affirmation cards, activity packets, links to videos, and links to illustrated books.

The materials are appropriate for, but not limited to, ages 4-12. They can be used with participants of any age, as they are made for children and inner children, as well.

The Children's Mental Health Toolbox can be found here:

https://namiwla.org/childrens-mental-health-toolbox/

About the Artists

Indy Rishi Singh is a regenerative farmer, healthcare advocate and an empowered educator. He regularly facilitates Neuroplasticity Playshops for corporations, schools, and communities. Indy loves to produce immersive experiences centering on regeneration and civic imagination. Indy studied medicine at St George's University and biological sciences at UC Davis, and is the Executive Director of the healthcare nonprofit Cultivating Self (www.cultivatingself.org). He is also certified in Mental Health First Aid, Ayurveda, Yoga Therapy, and Science of Happiness. Connect with Indy on IG at @ticklesaint , join regenerative eco-therapy projects at www.cosmiclabyrinth.world or listen to his podcast at on Spotify, "Political Hope with Indy Rishi Singh".

Oshri is a Los Angeles- based artist and musician. He is a children's book author and illustrator, creating books that touch on mental health, mindfulness, inter-being, and consciousness for ages 2-202. Oshri loves to generate creativity that aids people and communities in our individual and collective healing journeys. He studied psychology and management at Duke University, and is also certified in mediation and dialogue facilitation, and yoga instruction. More of his art can be found on Instagram: @oshrihakak .

More Books by Butterflyon Books
www.ButterflyonBooks.com

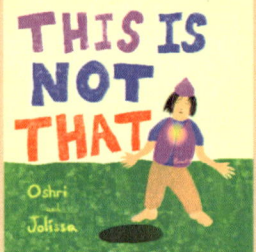

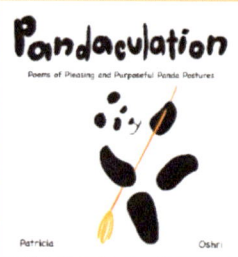

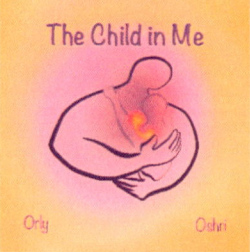

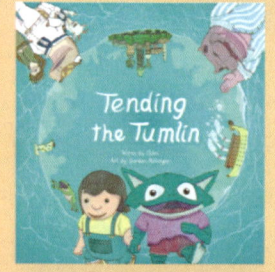

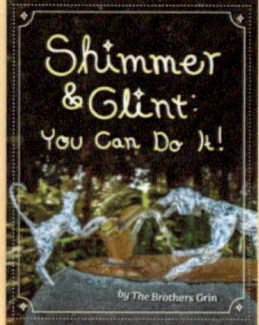

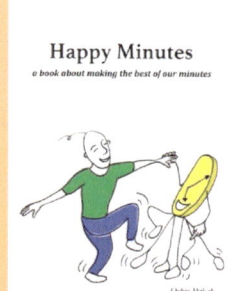

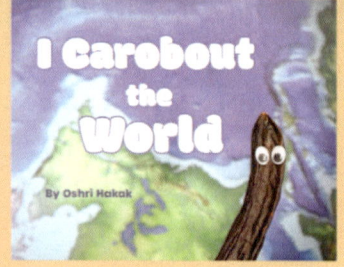

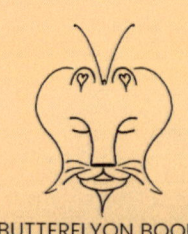

BUTTERFLYON BOOKS